W9-AVK-518

Life Is Like A
Ten-Speed Bicycle

by
SCHULZ

CollinsPublishers

A Division Of HarperCollins*Publishers*

Life
Is Full Of
Choices

Life Is Full Of Choices

Searching
For The Meaning
Of Life

LIFE IS A LOT LIKE A BASEBALL GAME

WE ALL HAVE CERTAIN POSITIONS THAT WE PLAY

WE ALL MAKE A FEW HITS AND WE ALL MAKE A FEW ERRORS

Blanket
Wisdom

A Packaged Goods Incorporated Book
First published 1997 by CollinsPublishers
10 East 53rd Street, New York, NY 10022
http://www.harpercollins.com
Conceived and produced by Packaged Goods Incorporated
276 Fifth Avenue, New York, NY 10001
A Quarto Company

Copyright © 1997 United Feature Syndicate, Inc. All rights reserved.
HarperCollins®, ® , and CollinsPublishers™ are trademarks of
HarperCollins Publishers, Inc.
PEANUTS is a registered trademark of United Feature Syndicate, Inc.
PEANUTS © United Feature Syndicate, Inc.
Based on the PEANUTS ® comic strip by Charles M. Schulz
http://www.unitedmedia.com

ISBN 0-00-649229-0

Printed in Hong Kong

1 3 5 7 9 10 8 6 4 2